Each of us is given the same number of hours every day, but some people make more things happen in the same time. Why is that?

Well, they have learnt an important, and yet mostly untaught, life skill.

They have learnt how to go from 'talk' to 'action'. They have discovered the secret of 'Doing'.

And yet, becoming a Doer is simple enough. It is a habit that we can all acquire.

This little book takes us through the simple steps that every person, every project, every business, will probably encounter on their way to making stuff happen successfully.

SET YOURSELF A GOAL.

(you can't score unless you have one)

SET YOURSELF A DEADLINE.

(don't make it too easy,
a crazy deadline can help)

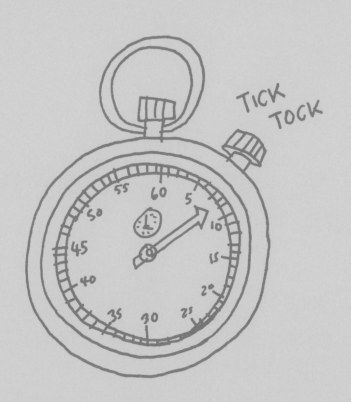

DEFINE SUCCESS AT THE START.

(money, happiness, saving the world...
   that sort of thing)

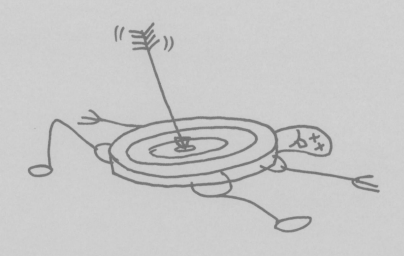

MAKE A PLAN TO MAKE IT HAPPEN.

(remember, most things fail
 because they never...er...start)

BUILD A TEAM TO HELP YOU.

(no matter how brilliant you are,
 you can't do it alone)

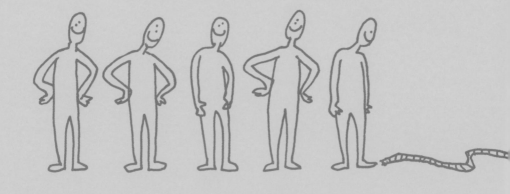

GET THE TEAM TO SIGN UP, HEAD AND HEART.

(tell them the dream, play down the bit about all the hard work, late nights etc.)

UNDERSTAND THERE WILL BE HURDLES, BARRIERS.

ACCEPT THEM.

WORK EACH DAY TOWARDS THE GOAL.

(obsession...ahh, the smell of it)

A LITTLE CAN DO A LOT.

(especially, if repeated, if repeated, if...)

EACH DAY IMAGINE THE DREAM AS IF YOU'VE ALREADY DONE IT.

(it may sound weird, but it will help)

UNDERSTAND THE IMPORTANCE OF YOUR ENERGY.

YOUR STUBBORNNESS.

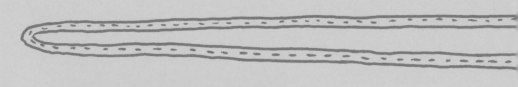

YOUR PERSISTENCE.

EVEN SO, HALFWAY THROUGH A PROJECT IS NORMALLY THE LOWEST POINT. YOU ARE NEITHER AT THE START NOR AT THE END.

(eek)

ENERGY DIPS. MOTIVATION SLIPS.

(double eek)

IT'S TIME TO REMIND YOURSELF
WHY YOU STARTED ALL THIS
IN THE FIRST PLACE.

(er...hello dream, you got a minute?)

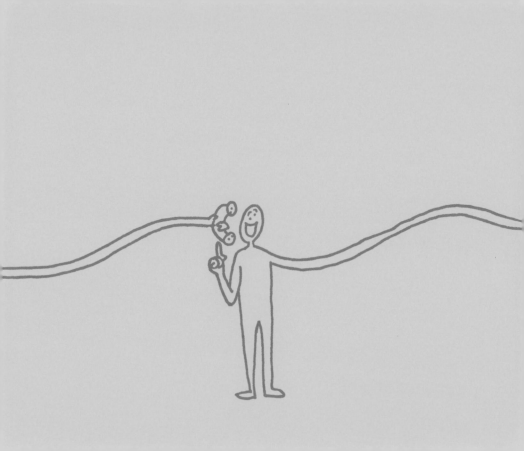

IT'S TIME TO LOOK BACK AT HOW FAR YOU HAVE COME.

(wow. no way!)

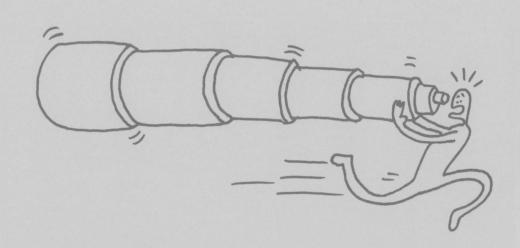

AND IT'S TIME TO GIVE YOURSELF SOME EXTRA MOTIVATION.

(sfx: BOOM)

SO TELL THE WORLD WHAT YOU'RE DOING.

TELL THE WORLD WHY YOU ARE DOING IT.

(even if they don't get it, tell them anyway)

AND TELL THEM YOUR CRAZY DEADLINE.

(let them feel your urgency)

YOU'VE PUT A LOT OF PRESSURE ON YOURSELF.

(that's not such a bad thing)

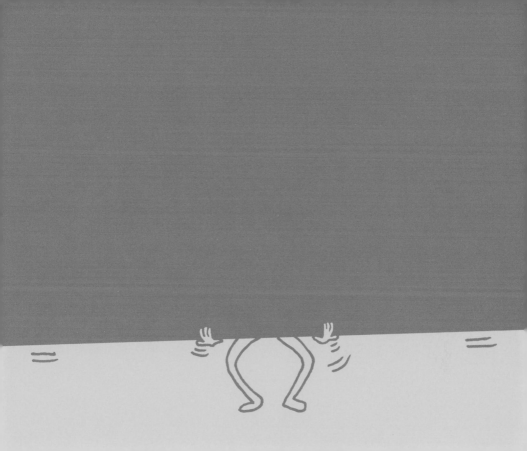

IT WILL GIVE YOU ENERGY FOR THE FINAL PUSH.

THEN ONE DAY, MANY, MANY MOONS AFTER STARTING, YOU FINALLY CROSS YOUR FINISHING LINE.

(yeehah)

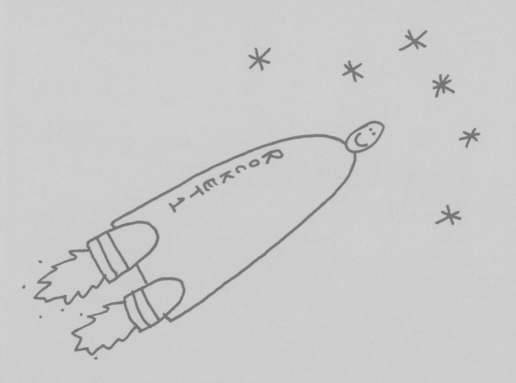

YOU'VE IMPRESSED A LOT OF PEOPLE.

(including that person called you)

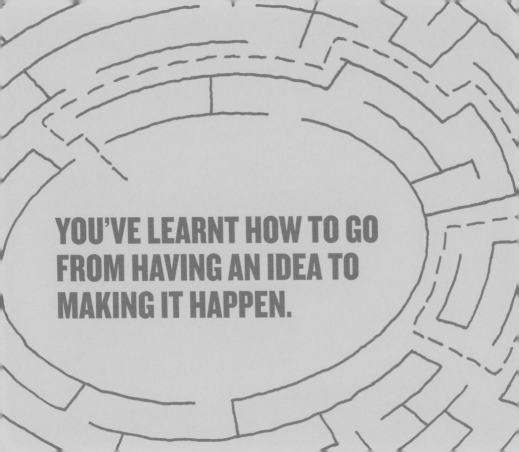

YOU'VE LEARNT HOW TO GO FROM HAVING AN IDEA TO MAKING IT HAPPEN.

YOU ARE A DOER.

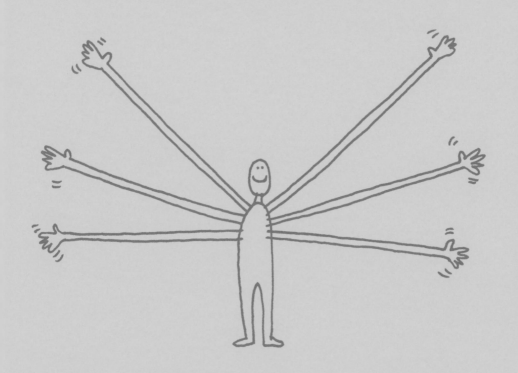

INSPIRING QUOTES

**Talent is the desire
to practice.**
Malcolm Gladwell

**A goal without a plan
is just a wish.**
Antoine de Saint-Exupéry

**Momentum keeps the stopping
away from the going.**
John Maeda

**I have been impressed with the
urgency of doing. Knowing is
not enough; we must apply.
Being willing is not enough;
we must do.**
Leonardo da Vinci

**People who say it cannot
be done should not interrupt
those who are doing it.**
George Bernard Shaw

The greater danger for most of us lies not in setting our aim too high and falling short; but in setting our aim too low, and achieving our mark.
Michelangelo

Don't just stand there, do something.
Dick Dastardly

There is nothing in a caterpillar to suggest a butterfly.
Buckminster Fuller

Whatever you can do or dream you can, begin it. Boldness has genius, power and magic in it.
Goethe

FUEL FOR THE JOURNEY

Books

As a Man Thinketh
James Allen

Choose Yourself
James Altucher

Design Your Life
Bill Burnett & Dave Evans

Do Open
David Hieatt

Do Purpose
David Hieatt

The Four Agreements
Don Miguel Ruiz

The Law of Attraction
Esther & Jerry Hicks

Let My People Go Surfing
Yvon Chouinard

Websites

dolectures.com

perell.com

swiss-miss.com

trends.google.com

hiutdenim.co.uk

Apps

Evernote

Instapaper

Planoly

Rev

Slack

Zoom

David Hieatt joined Saatchi and Saatchi at 21 years old. After a decade or so, he left advertising to build his own brands. He has built brands (howies, Hiut Denim, the Do Lectures) from nothing, with next to nothing, just by understanding a few basic rules. No big marketing budget. Just one email at a time.

Andy Smith is regarded as one of Britain's top illustrators. His client list includes some small but up and coming brands like Nike and *The Guardian*, etc.

His style is innocent, optimistic and humorous. From looking at his work, you get the sense that he is playing for a living, rather than working.